EBURY PRESS

TO, THE BRAVEST PERSON I KNOW

Ayesha Chenoy is currently the CEO and founder of one of India's largest independent digital advertising agencies, RepIndia. The agency has launched brands like Burger King and Gap on digital, and works with P&G, Canon, Suzuki Motorcycles, Fabindia, JSW, Tata Trusts, Adani Group, etc.

Prior to this, Ayesha had started India's first-ever wine investment fund and the first-ever dating website where only women could send friend requests.

Ayesha studied economics at Cambridge University, where in 2001 she was awarded the Adam Smith Prize for Economics, previously awarded to Amartya Sen. Post that she went to the London School of Economics.

She moved back to India in 2009 after a long career as an investment banker. Her only dream is to write.

To,
The
Bravest
Person I Know

AYESHA CHENOY

EBURY
PRESS

An imprint of Penguin Random House

EBURY PRESS

USA | Canada | UK | Ireland | Australia
New Zealand | India | South Africa | China

Ebury Press is part of the Penguin Random House group of companies
whose addresses can be found at global.penguinrandomhouse.com

Published by Penguin Random House India Pvt. Ltd
7th Floor, Infinity Tower C, DLF Cyber City,
Gurgaon 122 002, Haryana, India

Penguin
Random House
India

First published in Ebury Press by Penguin Random House India 2021

Copyright © Ayesha Chenoy 2021

10 9 8 7 6 5 4 3 2

ISBN 9780143452584

Typeset in Gandhi Serif by Manipal Technologies Limited, Manipal
Printed at Thomson Press India Ltd, New Delhi

www.penguin.co.in

MIX
Paper
FSC FSC® C010615

For Aari, Ivaan, Archit and Ishaan—to whom I owe my life

For Nainika and Nazneen—to whom I owe this book

And for each one of you, who struggles every day,
to become better, stronger

I owe you my words

A Note by the Author

I write this letter for you to give to the people you love, in the hope that my words will help them fight the feeling that they aren't enough and help them understand that everyone deserves love, that you are more than your mistakes, and that no matter what, you are brave, for just trying, to make it through the day.

Dear _____ ,

Why not write about
Rainbows,
Happy families
A candlelight dinner for two?
You depress me.
Lighten up, will you?

I am light.
My words misconstrued.
The storms, the fear, the darkness
I write about
Are my truth.
But what is also true
Is, I'm here
To tell my story,
Of overcoming darkness, finding light
Of the soul that made it through.

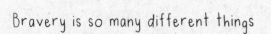

Bravery is so many different things

1

**I didn't fit
Into the family
Portrait.**

Struggling to fit in

'He only hit her once or twice,' Logic said to me.
'Once is more than enough,' said Fear,
'For me to last for eternity.'

When home doesn't feel safe

I'm sorry I flinched.
I didn't know
If it would be a hug
Or a blow.

And fear settles into your bones

Is that what you would say?
That it was only once?

You were struck by lightning once.

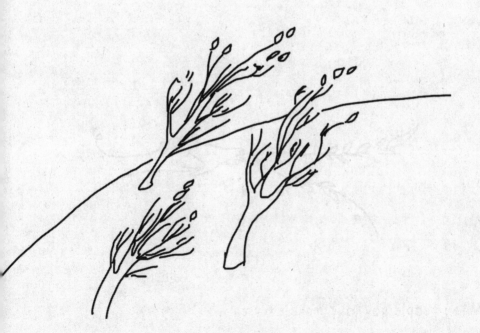

Never were more dangerous words
Spoken than 'but he loves me'.

When people you love make excuses

You planted the seed
I owed you;

You watered me sparingly,
Distracted by your oak tree.

The oak tree was diseased.
You chose to tend to
His need,
Forgot that I was growing,
That I needed your care,
That I was thirsty.

Now I'm a cactus,
Not the rose you planted,
You see.
My thorns would
Prick you
But I am the one that would bleed.

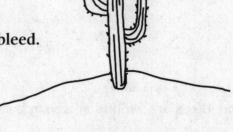

Oh mother,
Can't you see
What your martyrdom
Allowed you to be?
You were a victim
But so were we.
The excuse of your sacrifice
Was a death knell for me,
It was the reason you kept giving
For your emotional inadequacy,
Instead of taking your story
And setting us free.
Oh mother,
Can't you see?
You don't repeat history.

And there are victims all around, mostly you

You trained me
To walk on a tight rope
With strained nerves,
Fears of an impending fall.

And now you ask me
To be fancy-free,
To walk with reckless abandon.
How easily you change your story,
Expect that I will forget it all.

Your parents control your story

**In fulfilling your dreams,
I turned into my nightmare.**

And you disappoint each other

**You gave the
Fish everything
Except water.**

When all you want is to be loved and accepted

Jack and Jill
They fought for a bill.
All they wanted was a happily-ever-after.
But Jack was they and Jill was gay
And the world couldn't accept their laughter.

So Jack and Jill
They fought for a bill.
All they wanted was a happy ever-after.
But the world pushed Jack down,
Broke their crown
And Jill couldn't last much longer.

For who you are

Blood was thicker
Than water,
She warned me.

But what of blood that makes
You bleed?

Water was all I need.
Parched lips
Thirsty for love,
Drenched in his
Promise to me.

Blood was thicker
Than water,
She threatened me.

Then let me bleed out
And fill my veins
With water.
Your blood,
It's a curse.
Water will set me free.

And so you make your own family, of friends and lovers

13

Our friendship was a see-saw.
You were always up in the air
While I waited on the ground
For my turn to rise.
It's only fair.

But my needs were so heavy
And yours so light
That they weighed me down,
I couldn't take flight.

I know now
That the balance will never change.
I shall find a new partner
In life's little game.

With different needs

You walked all over this bridge;

You just didn't cross it.

Different expectations

She said,
'Call me if there is a storm.
I'm no fair-weather friend;
I know we never speak
But I'll hold you in the end.'

And days and years passed
And the storm came.
I couldn't remember her number
Or she my name.

You keep telling me to have
More boundaries, because you're
Scared I'll scale your walls.

And your walls begin to crumble

Tell me your sad stories,
And I will tell you mine,
And our pain will feel love
For the very first time.

Tell me your sad stories,
And I will tell you mine,
And in our pain will be a new friendship,
With words that start to rhyme.

And your pain is understood

I wouldn't call you a friend,
A word used so flippantly.
Would water be a friend to the sea
Or breath to a dying man?

When I see you in a room full of 'friends'
All I want is you, our laughter and a glass of wine,
When you are in pain
I am the one crying.

I wouldn't call you a friend.
That would be a lie
For without you
There would be no I.

Because sometimes the greatest love stories

**Sometimes the greatest
Love stories
Aren't of lovers.**

Are of friends

I had no words
To describe our friendship,
But then
You never needed any.

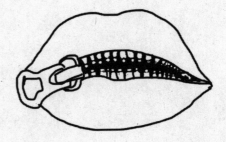

You insist on coming into my house
So you can keep switching off my lights.
No one invited you, my friend.
Take your darkness,
And your permanent night.

In this journey, people may bring you down

I trimmed my edges
Made myself small
Uncomfortable
By it all.
This puzzle I wanted to fit in,
It wouldn't accept me.
All its pieces
Beautiful, in symmetry.
So I found another puzzle.
I became a crucial piece,
Happy and wanted
And free to be me.

And you may well struggle to fit in

I was in the middle of a storm
And all you could ask was if
I heard your
Thunder?

Befriend those who have no space for you

You keep
Desecrating the grave,
Digging up dead pieces
Of me,

Pieces that hurt you,
That belong in a cemetery.

And now these pieces
Are poetry,
Asking for your forgiveness,

Asking you let them be.

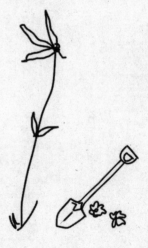

Who have their own demons

Her roses were more red,
Her violets more blue.
Truth be told,
It was because she had you.

And you may act unfairly

She gathered people like
Sticks, branches, stones.
'Pick me pick me,'
They longed for a home.

Some gave her strength,
Others beauty;
Some their weight in gold,
Others firewood
When the nights got cold.

And when the storm came
And their home lay broken

'She used me,' they cried
Together, holding hands.

Her home, their home,
Destroyed.

'You used us.
How could you?'

And she whispered,
'So did you.'

Feel used by some, and use others

I hated her till I became her.

Jealousy gets the better of you

We put her up on a pedestal and
Clapped the loudest when she fell off.

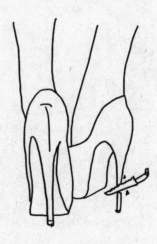

I handed you an olive branch
And you used it as firewood to burn
My house down.

You face betrayal

Anyone who thinks love is heart-shaped
Has never fallen in love.

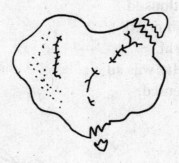

And when you go finding love

I burnt all
Your photos
And said a prayer
That the ashes would
Warn her,
Settle in her dark hair,
That this fire
Would burn
Your house of lies,
The embers lie cold
In your new lover's eyes,
Your flame doused
By the tears I cried.
Oh, this world,
Where loyalty was so
Callously denied.

You may find heartbreak instead

The space
Between
I love you
And I love you too,
I thought it would
Destroy me
Till I
Filled it with
You too.

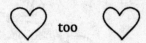 too

Or unrequited love

Dark magic was cast,
The witch captured
His heart.
A spell turned our castle into dust.
Memories of us
Were distorted by lust.
The touch of her wand drove us apart.

I drank the truth potion.
It shattered my notion.
It was him, not her,
The wizard,
His devious craft.

Infidelity

By the time
We got to my chapter
Our story was over.

Or narcissism

You loved the moon,
Chose her,
Pursued her,
Promised her the skies.
Time passed and you wanted her to change,
To come out only in the day
But be yours at night.

You covered her with dark clouds
Till she was invisible.
The world missed her.
Her eclipse was permanent hell.

Stifling control

He asked I
Develop a thick skin
So I won't
Easily bruise.
Instead, I peeled
Him off like
Dry skin,

Found a new muse.

Abuse

How can you control me
If you can't control your own self?
You wrote with a permanent marker
And now you want a different beginning
To a story that is near its end.

Find a new muse, a new story,
A protagonist you can control.
But even if you do,
The story may not change
Because nor have you.

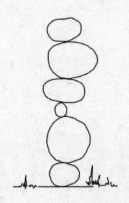

And it may take a while, but I hope you will

She hid under the leaf
And wouldn't fly;
The caterpillar
Who morphed into a butterfly.

I told her the truth
That this was abuse,
That she wasn't slow, or green
Or born to doom.

And she began to fly,
This beautiful butterfly,
With an anger that caused
A deadly typhoon.

Use that anger

39

You liked this shadow
She stretched for you,
Bent and long,
Obedient,
Tied to you.

But one day she changed.
Tired of this darkness,

She stepped over you.
She found light,
Joined the sun.
You found another
To follow you.

To rise

If you love the wind,
Don't ask
Her to change direction
Or be still,
Blow for your attention.

If you love the wind,
Let her meet the sky,
Let her fly unhampered,

Or love shall pass you by.

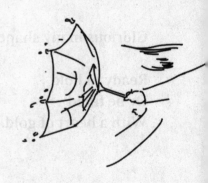

With the grace that I know you have inside of you

You moulded me
Like fresh clay,
Supple.
You had your say.

When you were done
You left me out to dry,
Washed your hands.
Bits of me to die
Hardened,
Emboldened,

Glorious in my shape.

Ready to hold
Or be filled
With a heart of gold.

To walk away

It didn't matter if you were hers
It didn't matter that we tried for years
It didn't matter that we didn't fit
You were always going to be my forever hit.

And it's natural to reminisce

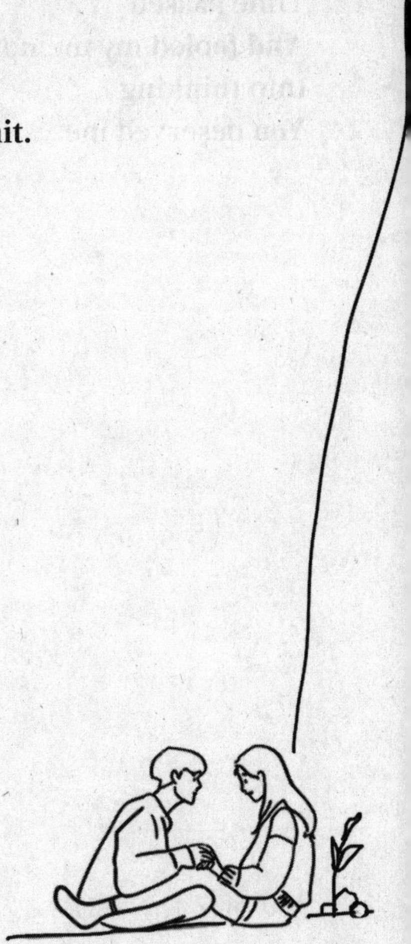

Time passed
And fooled my memory
Into thinking
You deserved me.

And pine for what

You asked that I
Feel less
Give less
Take less.

And when I did
You asked why I left you.

Was not good for you in the first place

She thought
He never looked back
Because he wouldn't
Miss her so.

He knew
He never looked back
Because she was always
In his mind
In his heart
In his soul.

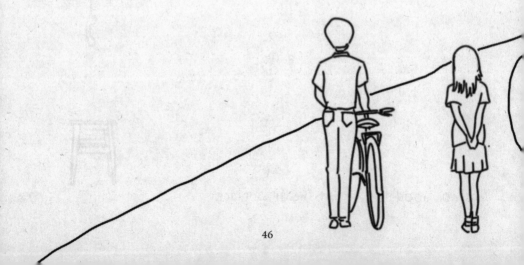

Everything before you was a lie.

And one day you will find love

The only hand I wanted
To be dealt was yours.

And

**The only uniform I would wear
Were your hands.**

It will

He tried to give me all the love they took,
And in that trying was all the love I needed.

You will always be someone's love song.

Find you back

My needs needed yours.

Your eyes were the only mirror
I ever cared for.

I tore off my skin
So I could be rid of your touch,
Gouged out my eyes
Blind to your beauty,
Gutted out my heart,
Every beat an ode to your breath.
But this soul
Tethered to yours,
It wouldn't forget.

An all-encompassing love

I would take your thunder
For a few drops of your rain.

I only ever noticed the wind
When it touched your hair.
I only noticed the sun
When it kissed your face.
I only noticed the rain
When it wet your lips.
I only noticed the earth
When it buried your body.

In this lifetime
I cannot repay you,
But the thing with the soul is, my love,
It remembers its dues.

'The one'

She lifted him with her pen.

'They pass right
Through you,
These compliments,'
He said.

'There's a leak:
Self-esteem,'
I said.

So he covered
The leak with his hands
And held me forever.
And in those hands was
The greatest compliment ever.

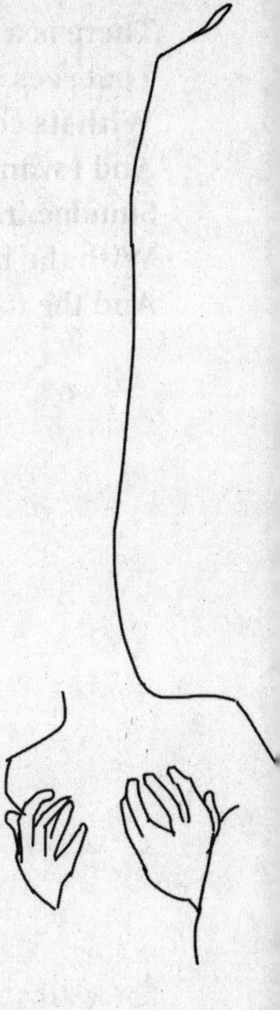

Who will love you

There is a small part of me
That sees a painting,
With its colour, its beauty, its symmetry,
And I want to touch it,
Smudge it,
With the blank ink inside of me
And the darkness of my poetry.

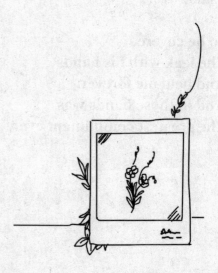

For everything that you are

What I learnt through hate,
You made me unlearn through love.

And everything you are trying to be

Many laid claim on you
Like you were a castle or country.
They would tell me of your dark dungeons
And the secret tunnels,
Your armies,
While they gloated, patronized me.
What they didn't see was that
The queen of hearts
Didn't need to know the king's history.

And there may be some that will begrudge your love

When you can't understand,
When you think I'm being unfair to you,
I want you to close your eyes,
Picture a little girl
Holding her broken heart
Asking you for some glue.

And you will struggle with old wounds

The stains wouldn't leave.
The name-calling, the blame.
My favourite shirt
Would never be the same.

Could we still wear it?
Was love a compromise?
I'm sorry we tore it.
It brought tears to my eyes.

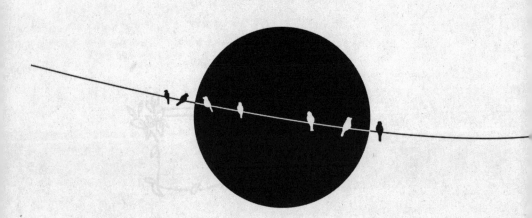

You may fight

You make me sick,
But you're also my
Only medicine.

And make each other so mad

All I could hear in our silences
Was the sound of you leaving.

And the insecurities will re-emerge as old wounds

I only threatened to walk away
So that you would ask that I stay.

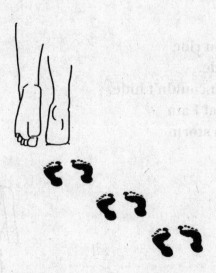

Not your jewel,
Your crown,
Not the gentle wind,
The tornado that shall
Blow you down.

Not the wave you ride
But the sea inside.
It was a love you couldn't hide.
Take me for what I am
For tempering a storm
Is suicide.

I hope that you will find compromise

If it had to be broken,
It would be you I
Would choose
Every single time
This heart was yours.

And choose each other time and time again

**The nightmares of you leaving turned
Into dreams of you returning.**

And try and make things work

I wish I had met you, after I met you.

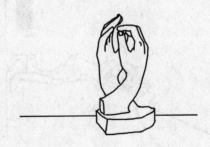

But sometimes, it just won't

All we had left was inertia.

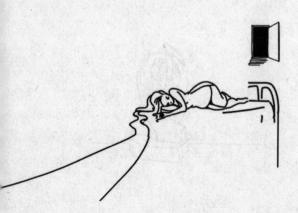

I found the
Letter you wrote me
When you left.
Your I's
Confident, leaning forward,
Crowding out the U's,
C's curled like our bodies in bed.

Distance between the letters growing,
Filled with words unsaid.

Blotted letters washed with tears
Love a four-letter word
Signed with fear.

No matter how hard you tried

Isn't it strange
How we started
And ended
Like strangers?

And this broken heart will have no choice but to mend

You didn't have to be something
For us to be nothing.

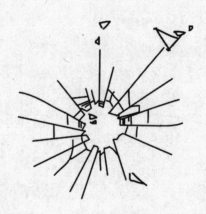

Because sometimes it's no one's fault, really

The greatest distances aren't physical.

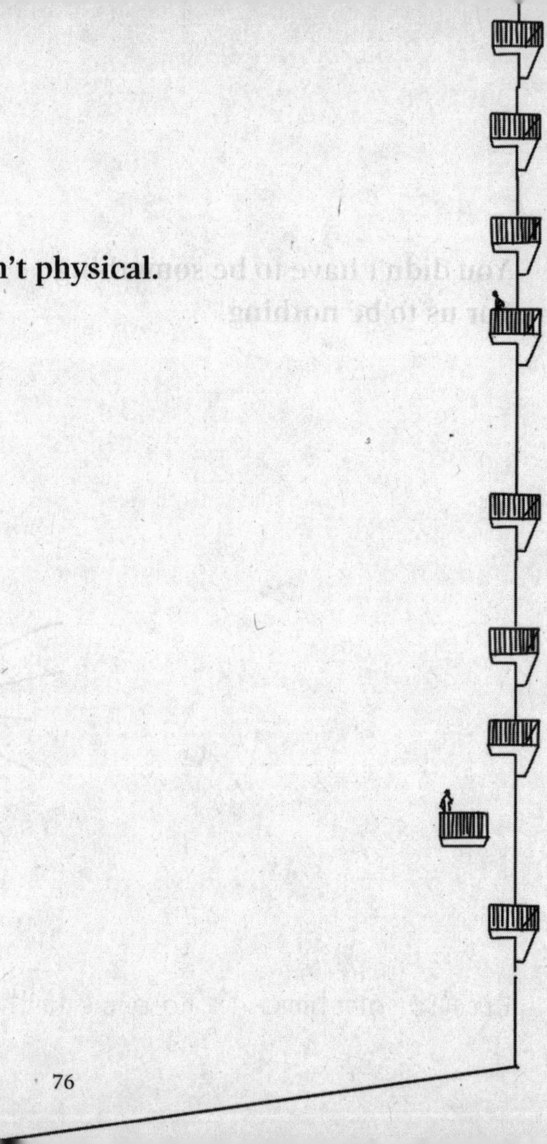

You took me
From
Alone
To
Lonely.

We just grow apart

After all these years
Destiny forced me
To stop playing hide and seek
To dance with my memory
To face the fears buried deep
To wrap my arms around my insecurities
To argue with my history
To accept my mortality
To love myself.
Alone would never again mean lonely.

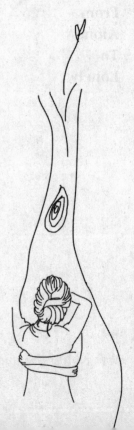

Through all this, I hope you will learn to
be happy in your own company

I would go to your past
And whisper in his ear
That some rainbows stay
And not all love hurts.

To understand
That god holds your tiny hand
That it was okay
That you are safe
That it was just a mistake

That I was there
Loving you from far away.

To be able to tell yourself, that it's okay

It was time to draw the line,
For in every second chance I gave you,
I lost mine.

To protect your gentle heart

Sometimes the toughest fight is giving up.

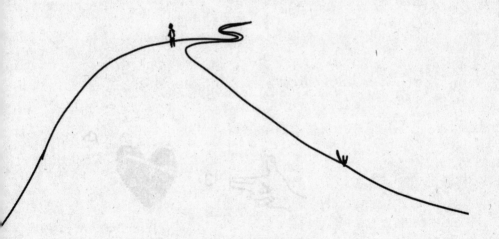

Know you've done all you possibly could

If the means were all that mattered,
We would only have good endings.

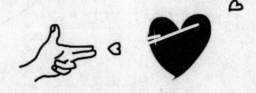

Understand that the journey is important

Even our lies had feelings.

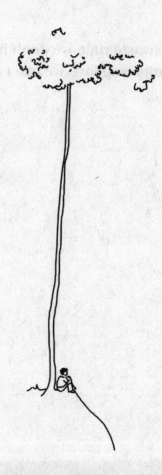

That you're more than your mistakes

We waste time we don't have,
Comparing love we can't measure.

$$\heartsuit = \frac{\heartsuit \; \heartsuit}{\heartsuit}$$

The sky told
The clouds to be less grey,
Asked the stars to shine less bright,
Showed the fleeting rainbow disdain.
She belittled
The shining sun.
Leave me alone, everyone.

They all forgave her
Disposition blue.
Everyone has a bad day,
Not just you.
So the rain washed her eyes,
The sun gave her a warm hug.
The rainbow stayed for longer.
All she needed was some love.

That we all have a bad day

I entered your story
A few chapters late
Enough to blur
Some lines of your fate.

I entered your story
At the cost of my own.
I gave it a better ending
So you won't die alone.

I swam in your seas,
You welcomed me,
Warm and salty,
Languid and free,
And just as quickly
You pulled me under.
I blamed your past,
You blamed my naivety.

Blame doesn't make things better

'It's me not you,'
Said the sea,
Like that would
Save me from
Drowning,
Like that
Would change
Destiny.

The picture you had of me,
That was only a mirage
For the world to see.
The one that was real
Was torn and blurry;
No frame wanted it.
It was dark poetry.

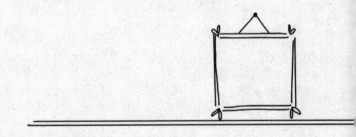

That even in your darkest times

Just start,
By being popular,
With yourself.

You're pretty damn amazing.

If I could just love you
In the way you need,
That is all
I want to achieve.
If that's the beginning, the middle,
The end of my story,
That I lifted you,
Your soul I could feed,
That's all
I want to achieve.

And you're enough, for me, for you

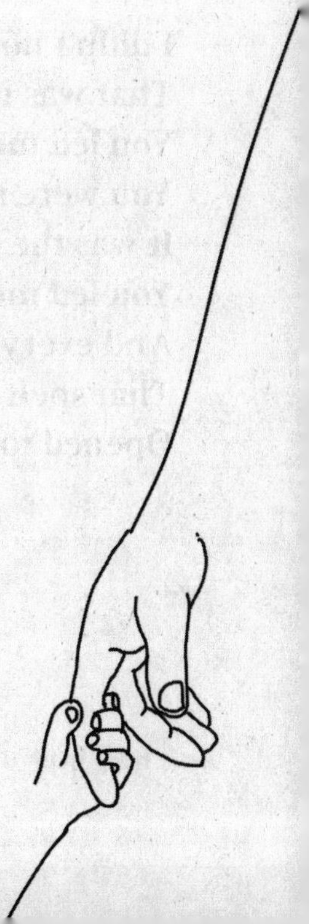

The door of validation was slightly ajar,
Tricking me,
Teasing me.
I spent my life trying to push it open,
No luck,
So far.

I didn't notice the other door
That was open and bright;
You led me away,
You were my light.
It was the door of love.
You led me through,
And every door
That spelt validation
Opened too.

That you are loved

Under your pillow I found devotion,
Under his, self-loathing.
In the sheets, a distorted love;
In the broken furniture was violence.
Behind the curtains, fear;
In the door, defiance.
I searched for validation,
I was starved for acceptance.
In your grave, I found forgiveness.

And I hope you will learn to forgive,

I knew I had forgiven you
When I stopped hoping
You got what you deserved.

When revenge came
Knocking at my door,
Her head bowed
Looking at the floor,
I wanted to turn her away,
Make her pay.

But I invited her in.
We talked over tea,
Her excuses turned into reasons,
My hate started to leave grudgingly,
And as her steps lightened
She morphed into redemption.
A reality dawned on me:
I had set us both free.

For that is the only path to healing

The storm tore her branches
But not the roots beneath.
The sky lost a star
But the sun gave her company.
You hurt me deeply
But love held me.

You see
Broken finds its own kind of happy.

And find your own happy

Why are you hiding?
My soul asked of me.
I like this darkness,
Said I, wistfully,
Where fear
Makes complacency easy.

Come into the light,
My soul said to me,
So I can touch your heart.
And you can be free.
And now I write
Uncontrollably.
Most other things
Mean little to me.

That you will pursue your passion

I kept waiting for the climax
Instead of writing it.

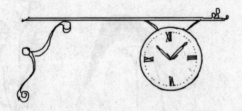

Even if it's scary

The laughter
With a friend
Who is now a foe,

The kiss from a love
That failed you so,

The sweat and tears
On plans that didn't fly,

Was it a waste,
Is it all a lie?

The laughter she
Remembers on her
Darkest nights,

The love
That helped him
Find his light,

The sweat and tears
They fed your soul,

Was it a waste,
Is it all a lie?

A ray of light,
A drop of rain,
The storms we battle
Enduring pain,

No love goes to waste,
No love is in vain.

With fewer regrets

You lived with regret
And I with you.

I was on my knees today
Knowing my voice
Wouldn't reach you
Any other way.

There was no shame
For in your hands
Was another soul's plan.

As for you,

One day you would see
That it wasn't me bending.
My soul danced free;

Yours learning humility.

With humility

I can't lie so I write.

Make friends with the truth

Is it only
Too much
If it happens to
You?

That you will learn compassion

I couldn't
Do as much as you.
I was fighting battles
Different from you;
Battles of a different kind,
Perhaps more selfish,
Never mind.

I couldn't do as much as you.
In the frontlines you fought,
You marched right through.
In spirit I was with you.
The things I posted;
I fought with family, friends
For this cause, your cause, our cause.
It may have seemed small
But it was all
I could do.

Not as large as you,
Not as brave,

But my heart beats for this.
I'm committed to you.
I couldn't do as much as you,
But don't shame me for the little I do.
Don't waste your weapons
By turning them on me.

Humiliation may not
Make me do more.

I'm already on the same side as you.

Be less harsh, even when others disappoint you

You were up in the sky,
I was on the ground.
You reached for the stars,
I reached for your hand.

You were up in the sky,
I would scream your name.
You were busy singing
The songs of fame.

I was up in the sky,
You were on the ground;
You reached for my hand,
Asked that I understand.

I was up in the sky,
I lifted you off the ground;
God smiled
As we held each other's hands.

**The things you do for me
Don't excuse
The things you do to me.**

That anger is only natural

If you could ask just one question,
Would it be,
How did you get here?
Or,
How can I help?

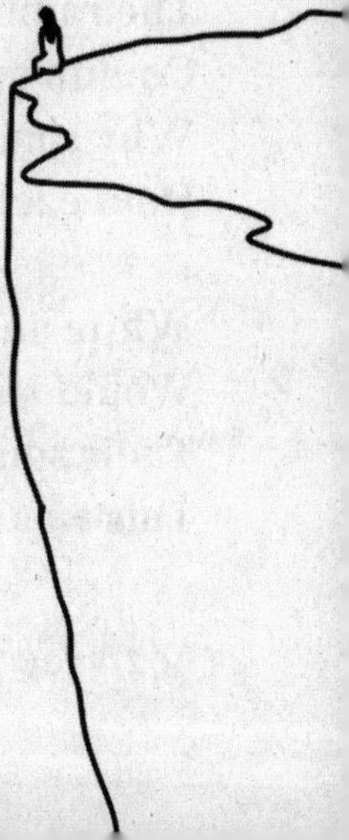

Be kind, listen

Did the rainbow
Tell you her story?
Of her colours,
Their mystery,
Of how white
Banished black
To the night,
The stars followed her,
Touched her darkness,
Gave her light.

The rainbow
Couldn't understand
Why shades of blue couldn't
Hold each other's hands,

White and black
Would still bleed red,
Their souls were one;
This was death.

The clouds thundered,
The rain tried to blur
This portrait of hate,
The colours of fear.

The rainbow,
Her heart broken,
Her appearance
Now rare,
She'd only come when the
Colours would love
Each other,

When god was fair.

And understand and accept difference

Save your silence for the funeral it caused.

Stand up for what is right.

Sometimes
You can only
Move forward
If you go back.

Reckon with your past

I stood at your grave
With nowhere left to go.

And even when you face loss

And the day came
When you couldn't
Remember what a
Rainbow was called.
'What is that band of colour?'
You asked me.

I thought that day the
Rainbow would
Forever disappear,

And then I remembered
How you taught me
To colour.

And illness

And as he
Looked for the moon
In the day,
The world thought him ill;
And I,
I admired his quest for beauty.

The only letters he didn't forget
Were those that spelt her name.

Memory

Watch helplessly as those you love suffer

Let me walk
To my grave,
Not stumble over pieces of me.

Don't drag me
Eviscerated
Down this carpet,
Red from a bleeding memory.

Don't take the light
From my eyes
That shone
On so many.

My soul pleads:
Let this body go.
Death with dignity.

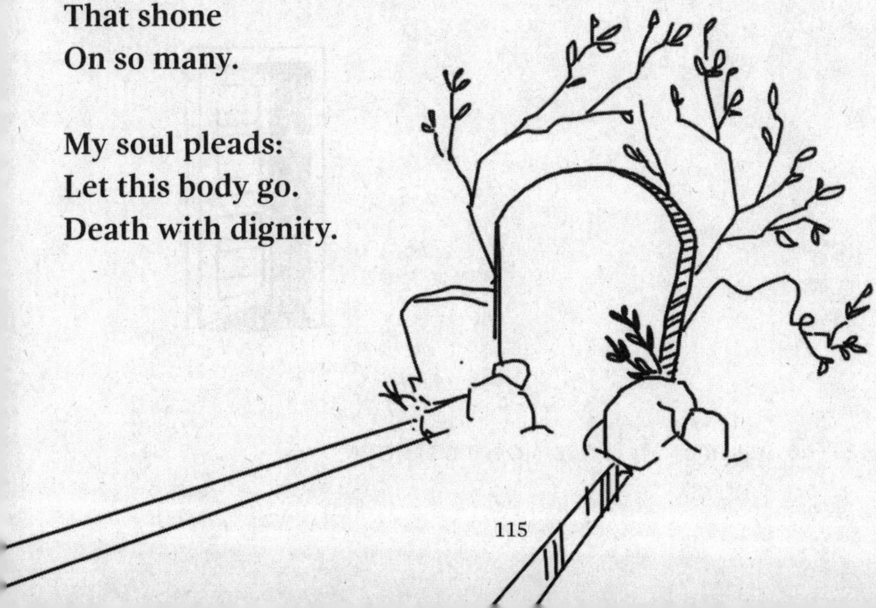

This too shall pass
Was my favourite saying
Till it came to you.

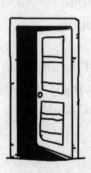

And face the passing of those you most love.

I dipped my pen
Into my memory,
Pricked the demons,
Made them bleed.
Bled out on to my pages
You called it beautiful poetry.

Be a stranger
To me today,
Pretend you
Know not
Of my history,
The battles that
I fight every day.

Be a stranger
To me today,
Averting your eyes
From the pain you see,
Your intimacy
Will bring me to my knees.

Be a stranger to me today.
Touch me not
Or this grieving
Heart will burst,
And tears will
Wash you away.

When grief is all you know

The only difference
Between you and me
At your funeral
Was that you were
Lying down.

One conversation between
Love and hate,
Luck and fate,
War and peace,

One conversation
To see differently,
To settle scores,

One conversation and
I opened the door,

One conversation
To let go,

One conversation
For us to know,

One conversation
Between you and me;

The difference between
Nothing and eternity.

And you're lost for words

I would lie to you
And say
I'm okay
So you couldn't lie to me
And say it would be.

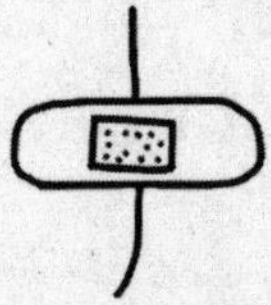

When it all seems like one big lie

Was I just a typo?

And nothing makes sense

How do you explain
To someone who has lost everything
That the eclipse is temporary?

Leave my pieces in peace.

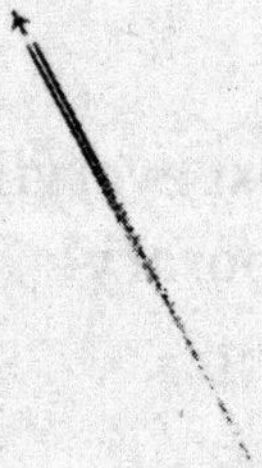

You want to be left alone

You said
You didn't believe
In life after death,
And then you left,

And I proved you wrong.

In all this I want you to know

He lived for tomorrow but died today.

That you have today, this one breath

You thought I had drowned
But really
I was lying at the bottom of the sea,
Holding on to his body,
My treasure chest,
Lungs filled with eternity.

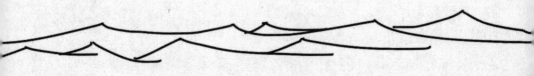

And you have me, and many others

Offers to listen poured in at her funeral.

And I am here to listen

Don't ask the sun for rain,
Make her feel like her light
Is in vain.

Let my words suffice,
My only vice,

For all this writer has
Is her pain.

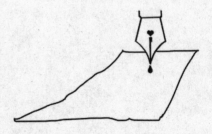

129

What kind of justice
Punishes the pen that wrote
About the wreckage?

That even when life may seem unfair

And when you write of love,
I hope no words do it justice.
And when you write of anger,
I hope your words seem like strangers.

And when you write of loss,

I hope you rely entirely on your imagination.

The light will always find you

You may not like
These marks of ink,

This dark poetry.

But these marks on paper
Were stolen from my wrist;

The only eulogy
I wrote for me.

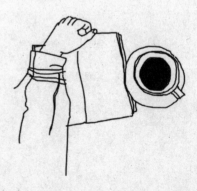

They say you've left
For a better place.

As for me,
Any place with you
Would be better.

On days
When my
Bed was a grave,

Would you say,
'You made it,
Lie in it'
Or
Would you
Tell me
How your sheets were
More crumpled,

More stained
But yet you
Stood brave,
Or
Could you
Just lie with me
Like a bouquet of
Flowers,
Commemorating
Everything life
Had taken away?

And it's brave to recognize when things get hard

It doesn't matter what
Pedestal you're standing on
If all you want to do is
Jump off.

That our problems are 'ours', not too big, not too small

What if
Your bucket list
Was
To not drown in it?

Even when it feels like you can't go on

When you
Reached out
Your hand
And she pulled
You under;

When you
Waited for rain
And only got thunder;

When everything
You built
Lay destroyed;

The love
You could
Never find
In your mother's eyes;

When hope
Is gone
And love
Is no more,

It's no wonder
So many
Drown near the shore.

I want you to know that it will get better

You would pick
Up pieces of
My broken heart,
Make them into art
Or medals of bravery,
Put them together,
Hand them back to me gently.

But what of my mind?
Were its pieces
Not worth your time?
You would look away,
Deny the signs.
The pieces had
No reason
In this perfect life of mine.

When would your heart
Understand
The battles of my mind?

Not now, not ever,

Till nothing was left behind.

No matter what they say

The thing with
A closed door
Is
Light can still enter
From under it.

It was time
I introduced
You
To
You.

You will always be

Brave to have fought the war,
Battlefields that are mountains,
Hospitals with the dead
Strewn across the floor.

We all have our own wars,
Our own battles ahead.

Sometimes bravery
Is of a different kind.
It's just getting out of bed
When your heart is broken
And demons bleed your mind.

The bravest person I know.

With love, _____

Acknowledgements

To Milee and the team at Penguin Random House India, thank you for taking a chance on me, for your support and your unrelenting faith.

To Nazneen, for reading and editing every piece in this book and the many that didn't make it; but more importantly for being my strength through everything.

To Vaibhav, for his illustrations and his vision. We made it this far.

To Nainika, for insisting I was a writer before we could spell; for her belief in me when I had none; for being my person, in a world I struggle to understand.

To Tarini, Ameeta, Jaiwant, for being more family than most families.

To Patricia, Prem, Bori, Neelum, Amit, Gauri, Karishma, Sam, Gaurav, Rahul, Preeti, Armana, Roshini, Kanika, Shagun, Natasha, Sumaya, Simran and my countless friends—you carry different pieces of me to the finishing line.

To Sameer Sain, for his unwavering faith in me.

To my team at RepIndia, for giving me the support I needed to write and for cheering me on every step of the way.

To my Instagram family, for all your love.

To my parents, who are in equal parts sky and lightning. And to Ritu Massi, for being my wise guru and surrogate mother.

To my brother, Archit, my other half, who holds my heart in his gentle hands.

To my husband, Ishaan, for making me believe in love and that it can last forever.

To my children, Aari and Ivaan, who are my hope, my reason.